How to use this book

Follow the advice, in italics, given for you on each page.
Support the children as they read the text that is shaded in cream.
***Praise** the children at every step!*

Detailed guidance is provided in the Read Write Inc. Phonics Handbook

9 reading activities

Children:
Practise reading the speed sounds.
Read the green, red and challenge words for the story.
Listen as you read the introduction.
Discuss the vocabulary check with you.
Read the story.
Re-read the story and discuss the 'questions to talk about'.
Read the story with fluency and expression.
Answer the questions to 'read and answer'.
Practise reading the speed words.

Speed sounds

Vowels

Say the sounds in and out of order.

a	e	i	o	u	ay	ee	igh	ow
	ea				a-e	ea	i-e	o-e
					a	e	i	oa
					ai	y	y	o
					aigh			

oo	oo	ar	or	air	ir	ou	oy	ire	ear
u-e			oor	are	ur	ow	oi		
ue			ore		er				
ew			aw						

Each box contains one sound but sometimes more than one grapheme. Focus graphemes are ***circled****.*

Green words

Read in Fred Talk (pure sounds).

boat sound down white cold beach woke safe home

huge* use* blue knew* new* blew few* flew grew

drew crew threw newt* stew* phew* brew chew

Read in syllables.

mot`or reall`y

Tues`day* news`pa`per* An`drew Stew`art* con`fuse* a`muse*

Read the root word first and then with the ending.

hard → harder big → bigger close → closer

late → later gentle → gently rescue* → rescued

carry → carried

*Pronounce ew/ue as 'oo' whilst reading this page

Red words

great brother above where could was what here someone through another there school water

Challenge words

wetsuit eye

Andrew

Introduction

Have you ever been to the sea side and played in a blow up boat? They can be good fun but quite dangerous as you can float out to sea. What would you do if that happened to you?

Andrew goes to the beach with his big brother. He decides to try out his new blow-up boat. One minute he is bobbing about in the sea, listening to the gulls and the next minute... he's in terrible trouble.

Will he be rescued?

Story written by Gill Munton
Illustrated by Tim Archbold

Vocabulary check

Discuss the meaning (as used in the story) after the children have read each word.

	definition:	**sentence/phrase:**
cool bag	*a bag that keeps food cold*	*We took a picnic in a cool bag...*
sand dunes	*small sandy hills by the sea*	*...and sat on the sand dunes.*
bobbed	*moved*	*My boat bobbed gently up and down.*
confused	*in a muddle*	*When I woke up, I felt confused. Where was I?*
shore	*the beach*	*I knew I was too far from shore.*
crew	*people who work on the boat*	*One of the crew threw me a lifebelt.*
deck	*outside walking area on a boat*	*He carried me up a ladder to the deck.*

Punctuation to note in this story:

1. *Capital letters to start sentences and full stops to end sentences*
2. *Capital letters for names*
3. *Exclamation marks to show anger, shock and surprise*
4. *'Wait and see' dots...*
5. *Speech marks*

Andrew

Tuesday June 28th

The first day of the school holidays.
I went to the beach with my big brother Stewart.

It was a day I knew I'd never forget.
A day when I was a fool.

We took a picnic in a cool bag and sat on the sand dunes.
We had a great view of the smooth blue sea,
and we were both in a good mood.

Stewart started to read his newspaper, and left me to amuse myself. I took my new blow-up boat down to the sea.

I lay in my boat, listening to the sound of the waves. A few noisy seagulls flew above my head, swooping to catch fish. My boat bobbed gently up and down, up and down ...

When I woke up, I felt confused.
Where was I?

The wind blew much harder now...
The waves grew bigger, and bigger,
all the time ...

Water slopped into my little boat, and my legs felt wet and cold.

I looked for Stewart, but I could only just see the beach.
I knew I was too far from shore.

I was really scared now.
What if my boat sank?
Or what if I floated here for ever?

Then someone shouted, "Andrew! Andrew! Can you see me?"

A motorboat – red, white and blue –
was bumping through the huge waves.

It drew closer.
It hooted its horn.
It was a lifeboat!

Phew! I was going to be rescued, at last.

One of the crew threw me a lifebelt
and told me to put it on.

Another man jumped into the water
and swam out to me.
He looked like a newt in his black wetsuit.
He pulled me to the lifeboat
and carried me up a ladder to the deck.

We were soon back on shore.

Mum and Dad were there – and Stewart.

Mum had given him a good telling off

for not looking after me.

The lifeboat crew had brewed up some hot tea.

Dad unscrewed the flask and filled a mug for me.

Later, safe at home, Mum gave me some hot stew. As I chewed the meat, I was thinking how stupid I'd been. I couldn't put all the blame on Stewart.

I was thinking that we both needed a set of rules,

to keep us safe in the water.

Rules for swimming in the sea

1 Don't swim straight after eating.

2 Don't swim alone. Don't let children out of your sight.

3 Don't use blow-up toys on a windy day.

4 Get out of the water if you feel too cold.

5 Keep an eye on the tide.

6 Look out for red flags. They mean "No swimming".

Questions to talk about

Re-read the page. Read the question to the children. Tell them whether it is a **FIND IT** *question or* **PROVE IT** *question.*

FIND IT

✓ *Turn to the page*

✓ *Read the question*

✓ *Find the answer*

PROVE IT

✓ *Turn to the page*

✓ *Read the question*

✓ *Find your evidence*

✓ *Explain why*

Page 9:	PROVE IT	*How do you know Andrew is writing about an extraordinary day?*
Page 10:	FIND IT	*What does Andrew do while Stewart reads the paper?*
Page 11:	PROVE IT	*What had happened to Andrew? How do you think he felt?*
Page 12:	FIND IT	*Who rescued Andrew?* *How do you think the lifeboat knew Andrew needed to be rescued?*
Page 13:	PROVE IT	*Why was the rescuer wearing a wetsuit?*
Page 14:	PROVE IT	*Who does Andrew blame for getting lost at sea?* *What do you think he said to his mum?*
Page 15:	PROVE IT	*How would you make sure people knew about Andrew's rules?*

Questions to read and answer

(Children complete without your help.)

1. What did Andrew and Stewart take to the beach?

2. What had happened to Andrew while he was asleep?

3. Who saved Andrew?

4. Why was Stewart told off?

5. Why did Andrew write a set of rules for swimming in the sea?

Speed words

Children practise reading the words across the rows, down the columns and in and out of order clearly and quickly.

Tuesday	holidays	amuse	gently	carried
white	new	threw	knew	newspaper
drew	chewed	great	brother	could
through	another	someone	many	their